The
Book of Love

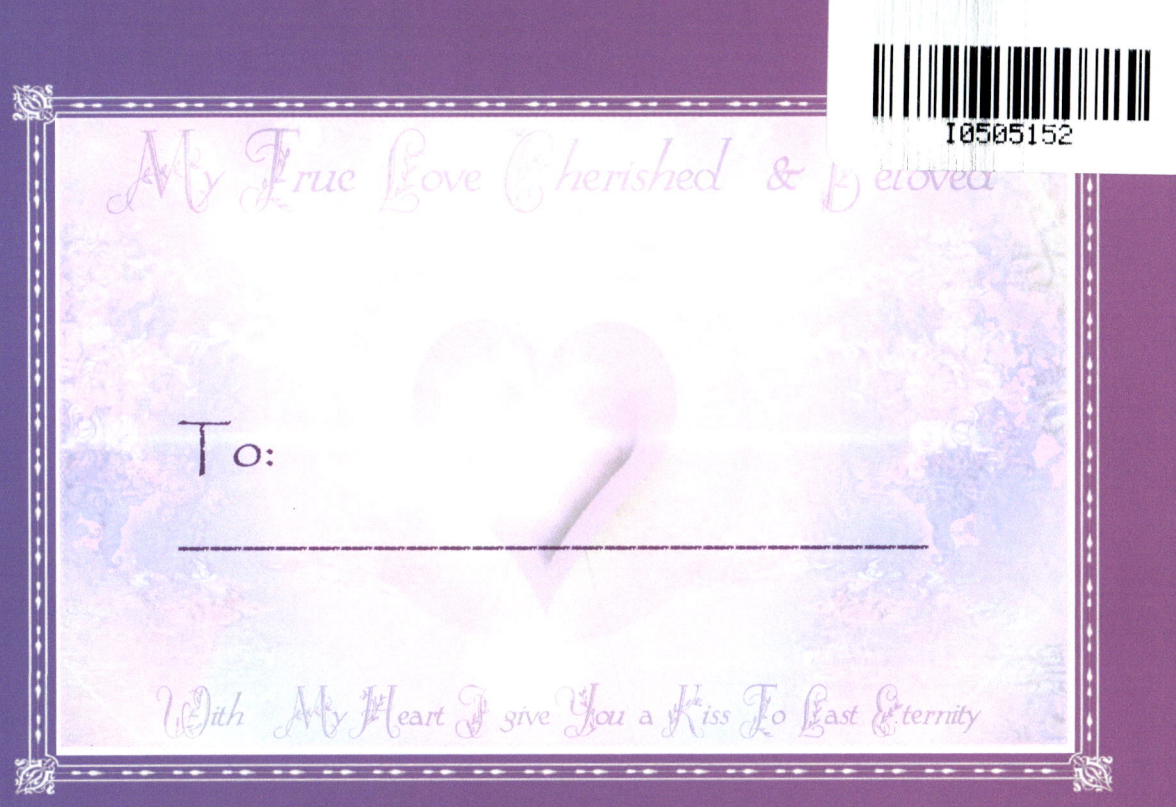

My True Love Cherished & Beloved

To:
_____

With My Heart I give You a Kiss To Last Eternity

Hearts of Love Artwork & Poetry

ARTWORK BY ALIXANDRA MULLINS

POETRY CONTRIBUTED BY SEQUOIA RAVENMOON,
GREGORY MULLINS & JENNI BOVETTI

This book is dedicated to
William Scott Poling, and William Ariel Poling,
my husband, my son - my loves. - Alix

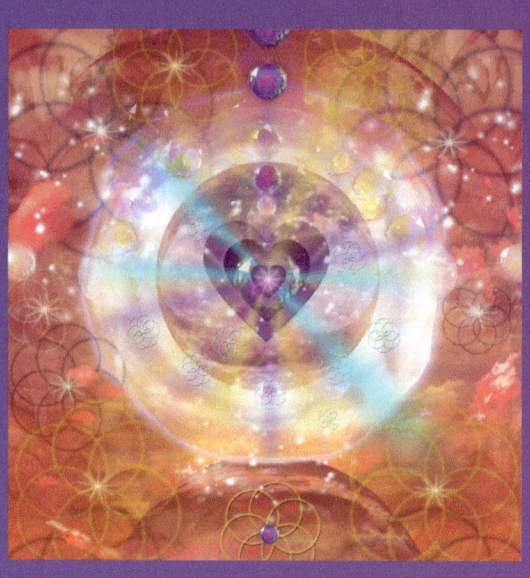

The Book of Love: Artist Series of Hearts of Love & Light

The art images included in this book are part of an on-going Artist Series revolving around the theme of love & the interconnectedness of all creatures. The concept of light connecting the human spirit to the spiritual realme, is universal and found in many of the worlds major religions. As an artist, I personally visualize the mystical universal love or "emotional concept" which is found in the world's major religions as a heart glowing with light. These images were created as my own personal visual meditations and artistic procress to manifest heart intention and, to focus on love energy. "Kevanah Ahava", "Kevanah" is the Hebrew for a spiritual focus or intention and "Ahava" is the Hebrew word for Love . Inspirations for the Hearts of Love Artist Series comes from meditations related to opening up the Heart Chakra (Heart Center) in your body, mind and soul. The intention behind this art is to manifest loving energy into lives and the world around you. Through enjoyment of these images and the poetic words, may they help you visualize love for yourself. Whether that means true love, compassion for animals, or simply appreciating the loved ones and beings in your life who bring you joy, it is open to interpretation.

- Alixandra

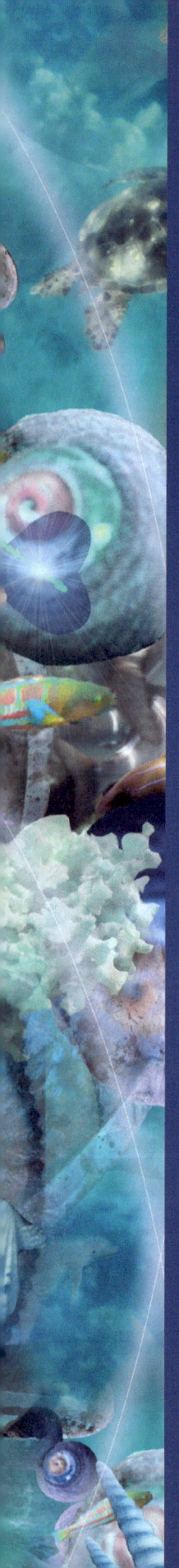

Waves

Warm Ocean waves
Salty Bliss
Sending Love
Never ending Kiss

An Ocean
of Love crashing
flowing, returning always

Tranquil Waters to you

- Alixandra Mullins

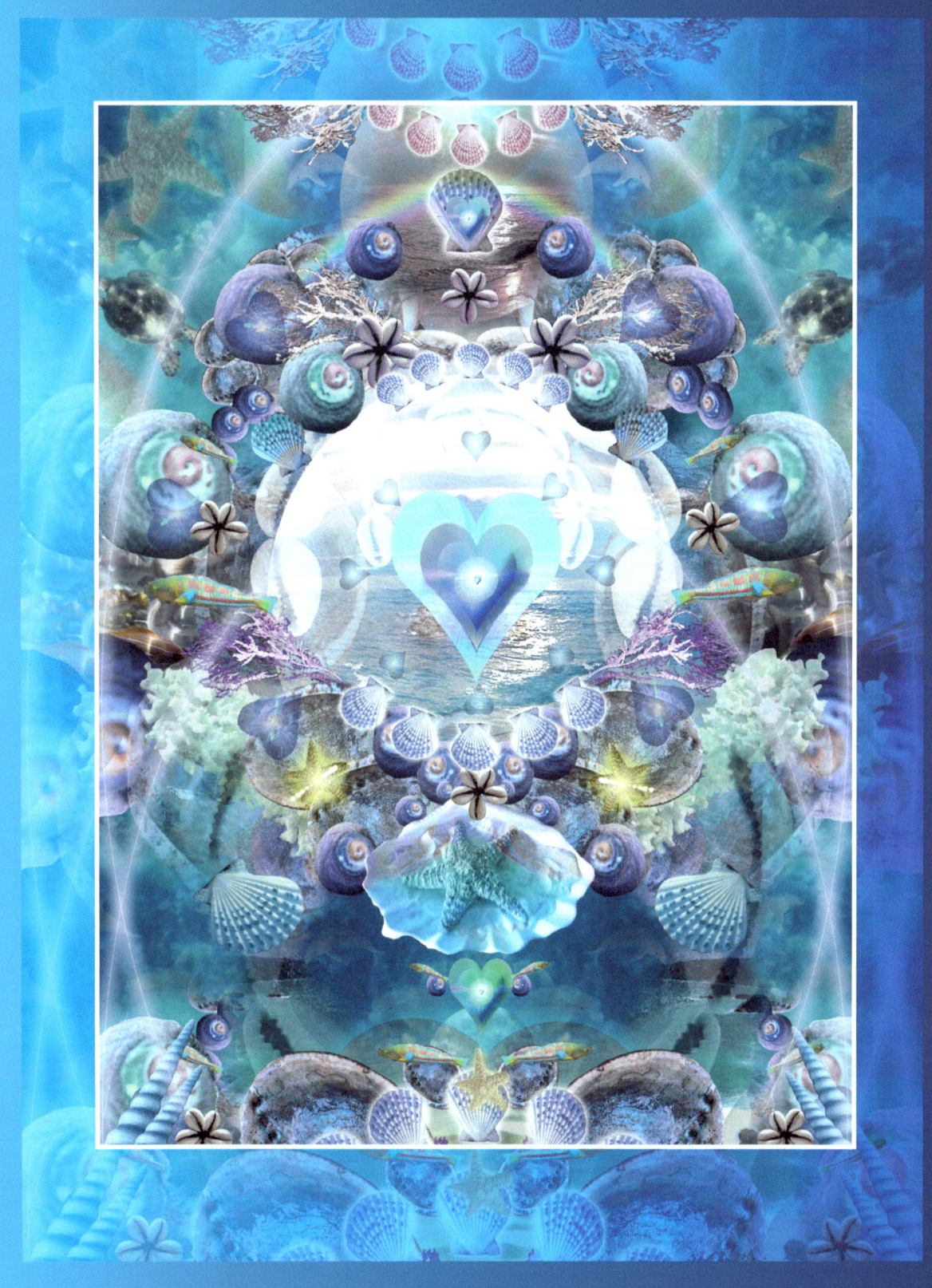

element: Water

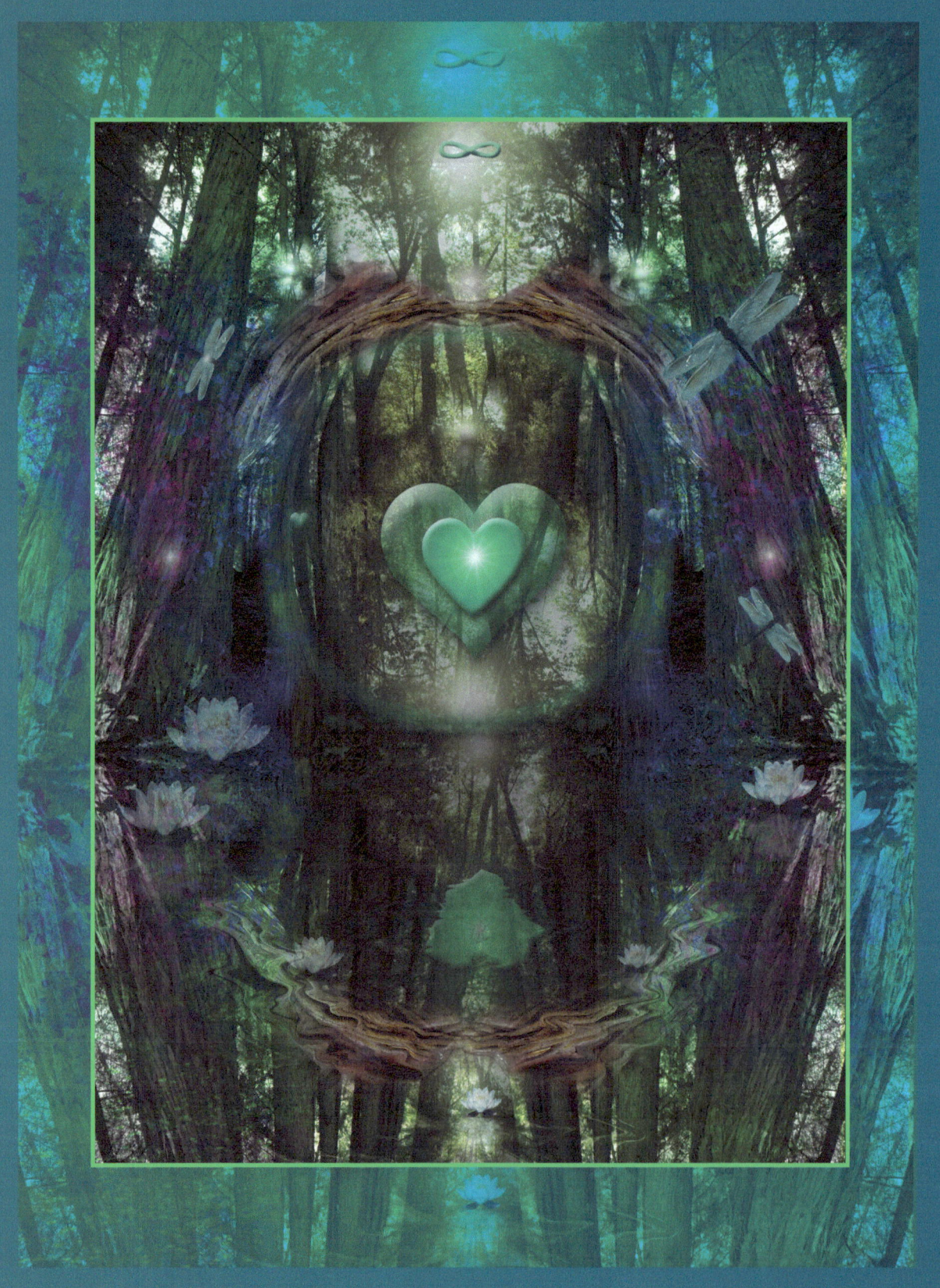

element: Earth

The Light in the Forest

Love exists

Outside Eternal

In the Ancient Forest

The Tree Tops hide the Sun

blocking out the Light

from Treasures of the One

Remember that the Sun

Still Shines its Light

Even on the Darkest Days of the

Ancient Forest Night

You are not Alone

-Alixandra Mullins

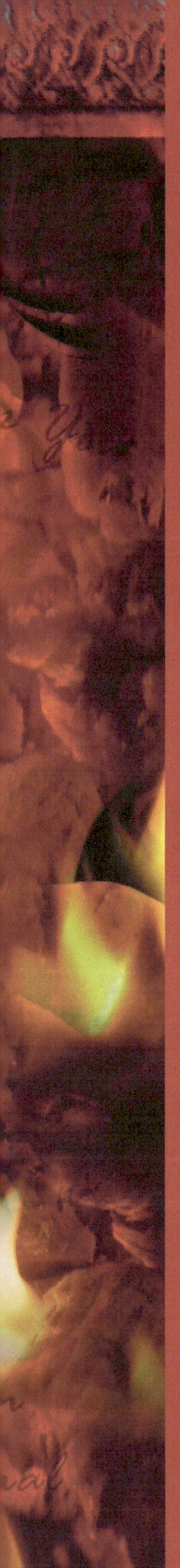

FireHeart

Ancient Fires

Light the Heart

Sacred Flame's

Eternal Dance

Raw Passion

Ignite

Burning Bright

Roaring Fires hiss

Ancient Sacred Flame

Burning Brightly

Passion Eternal

-Alixandra Mullins

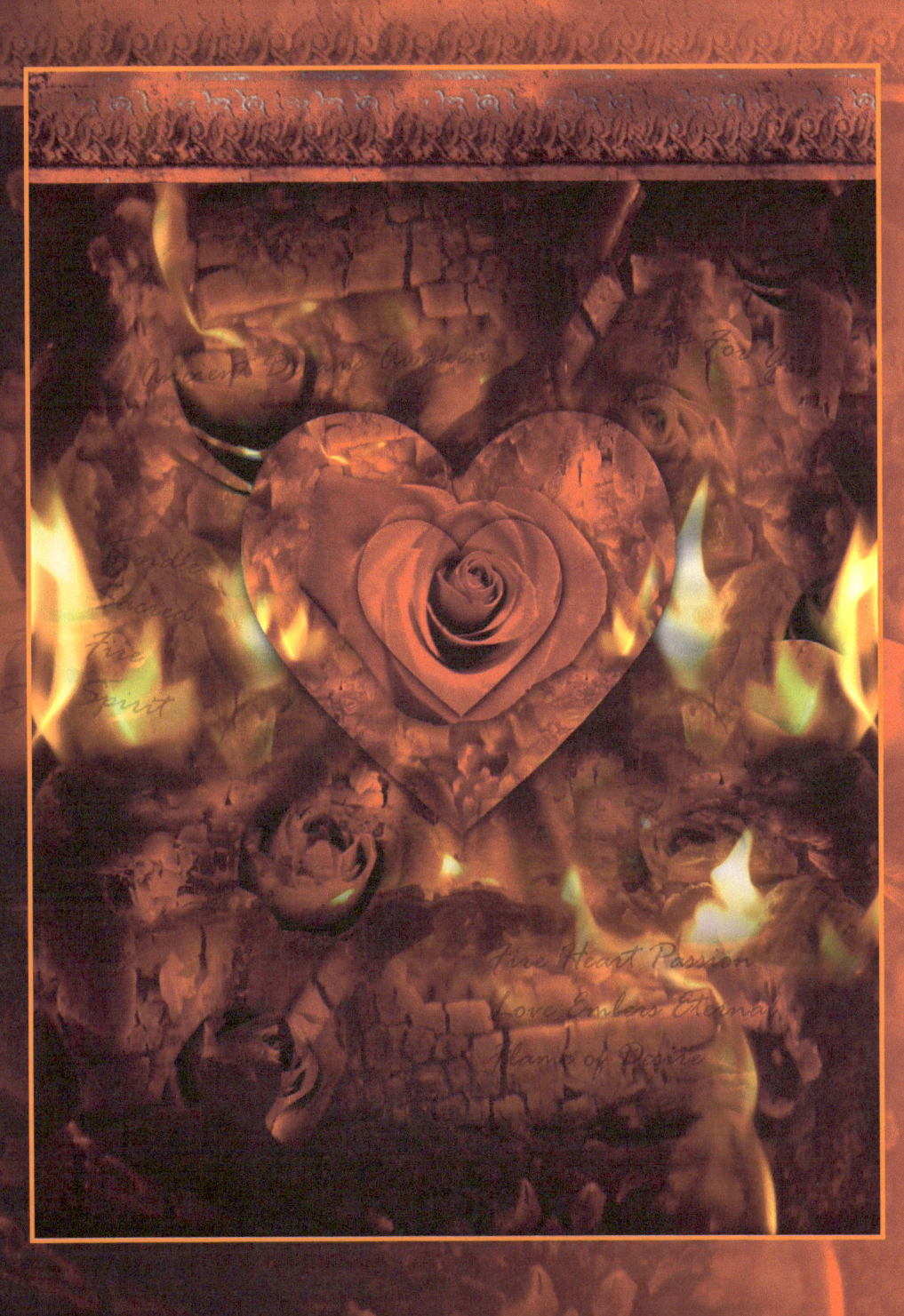

element: Fire

Lovesong

Love is a song

that words cannot sing

it sparkles more brightly

then bedazzled diamond rings

it grants joy to the old

and tears to the young

Love purer then gold

when two hearts become one

— Gregory Mullins

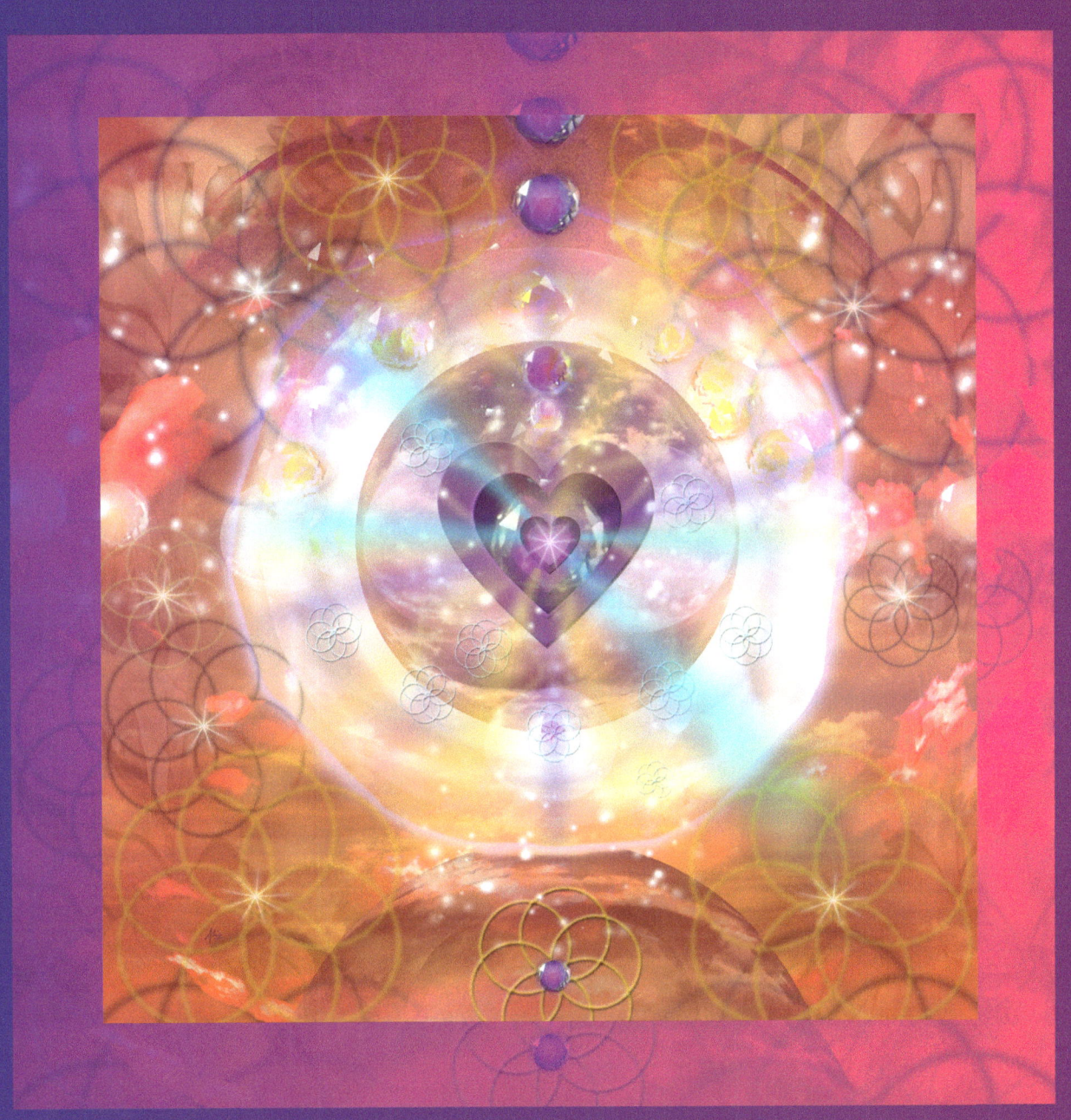

element: Air

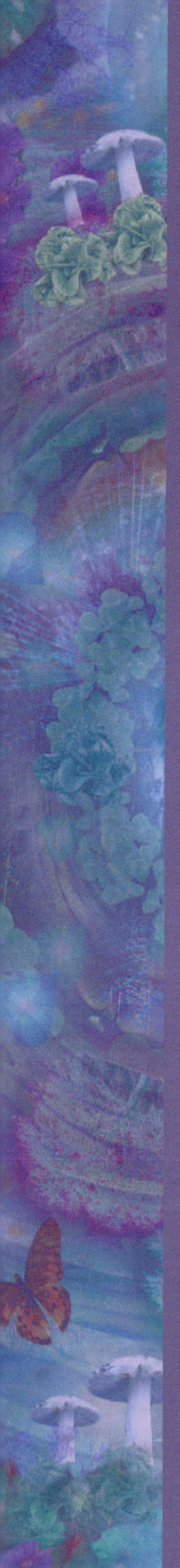

Heart of the Forest

Immerse Yourself

in Wild Leaves

of Nature's bliss

True Love found sweetly

underneath Nature's Trees

by Alixandra Mullins

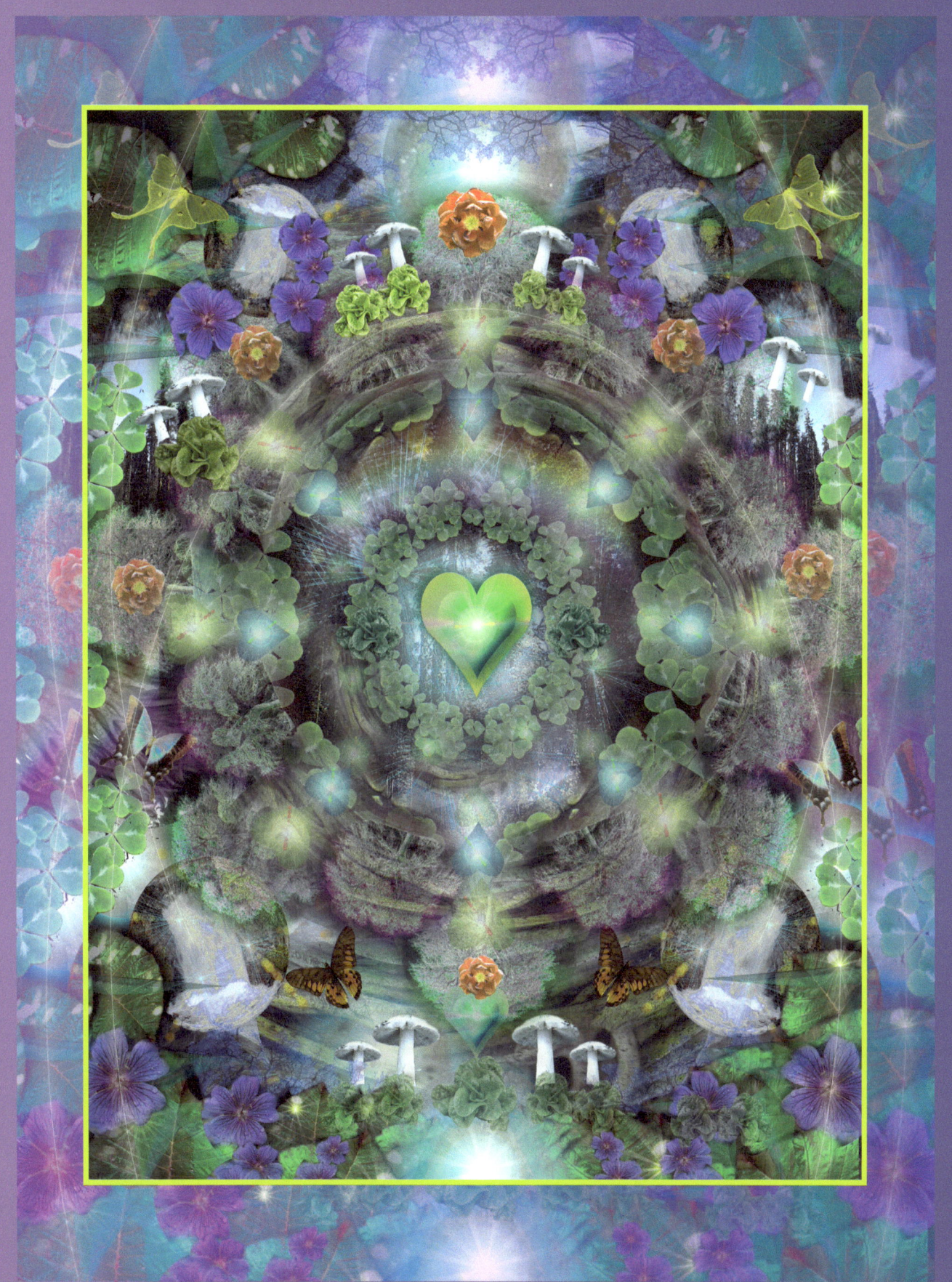

Flowergarden

In the Garden ,
my Beloved,
there i shall wait
till the sun sets
and the moon shines
there i shall wait
with no water
and no bread
there i shall wait
till you come to me,
Lover-
till you come to my tent:
till you come to me
my Beloved,
ever shall i wait.

- Gregory Mullins

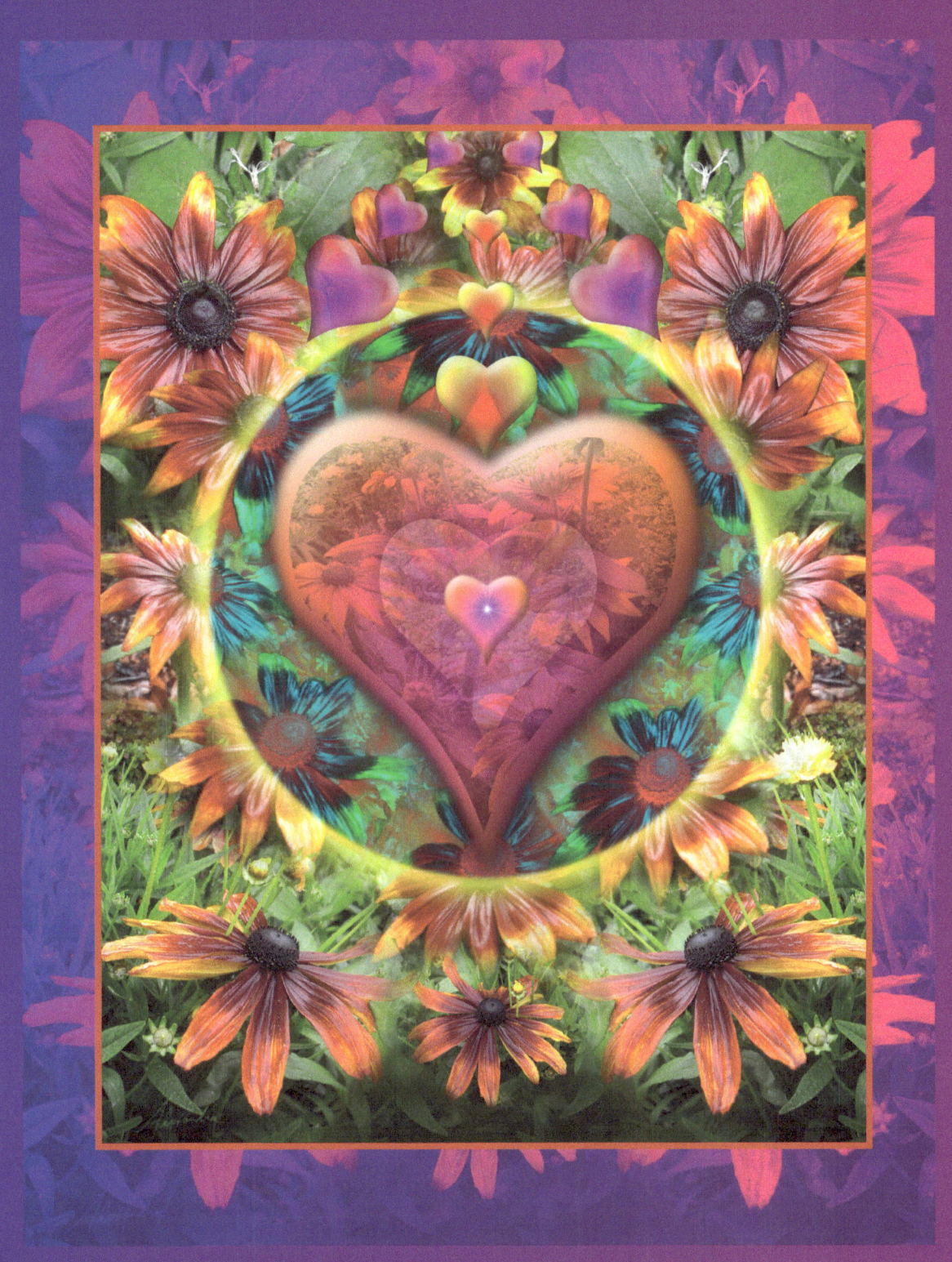

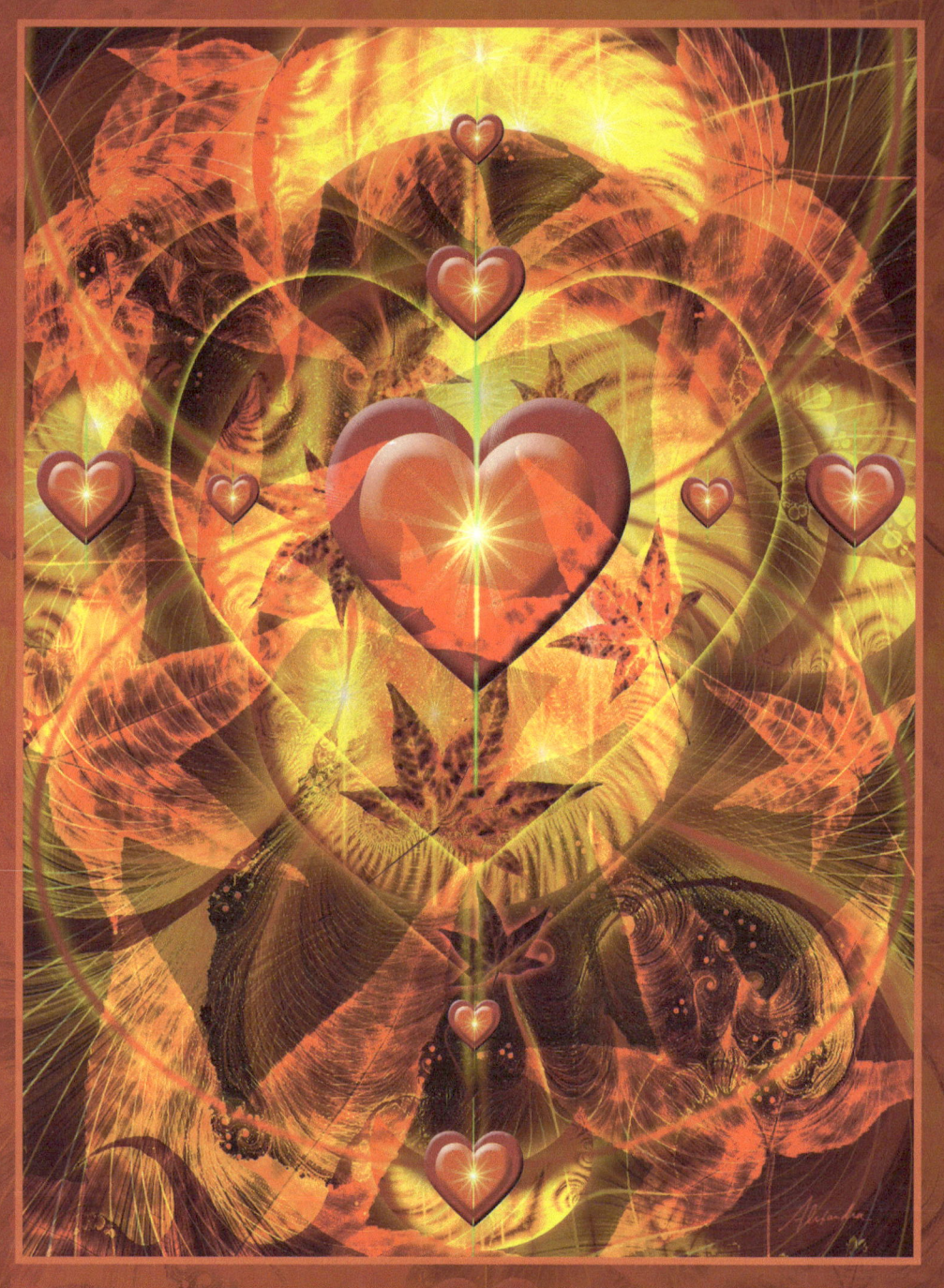

Love
a word
a song
a dream
Love
a feeling
warm like cocoa
sweet and soft
Love
makes all troubles
fade away
like clouds before the sun
Love
is more important
then bread or water
believe it
Love
is the best medicine
for all that ails you
I know it
Love
is in my heart, for you
and all people, great and small, friend or stranger.
Love is the soul of mankind.

- Gregory Mullins & Jenni Bovetti

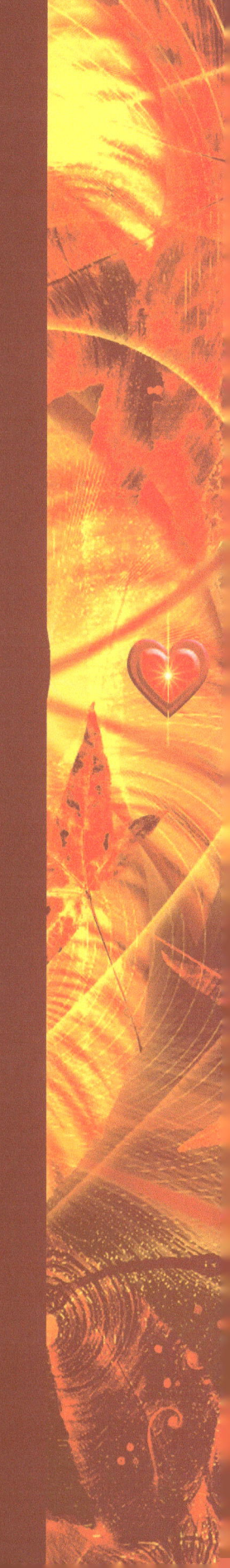

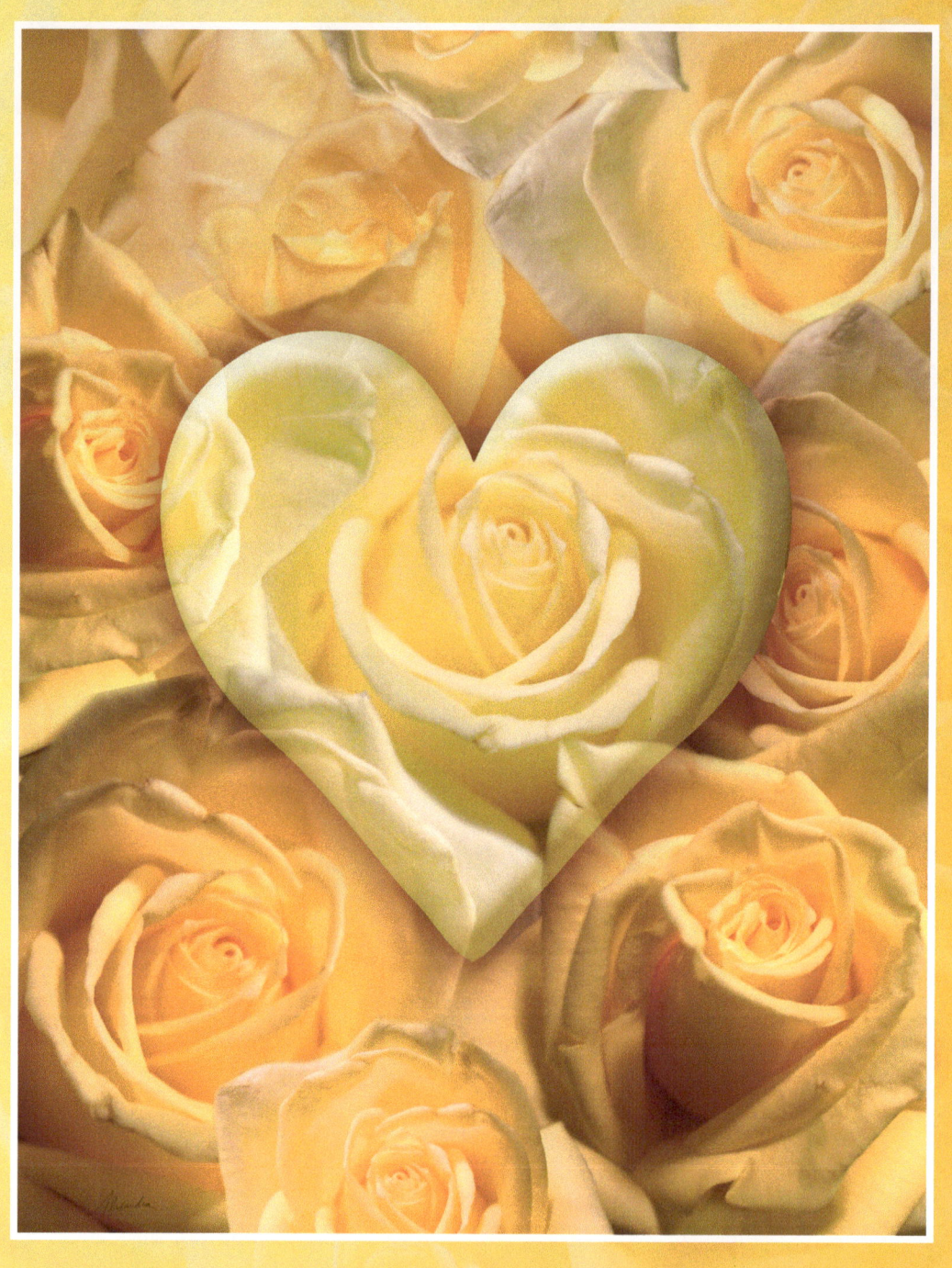

LoveFlower

Love is a like a flower
Love is like the ocean blue
Love is in every hour
That I spend time with you

In your eyes there is a sparkle
bright like a thousand suns
I could sit with you through darkness
until the morning comes

On this path of love we travel
knowing not where it may lead
Holding hands together
Love is truth in word and deed

The Beloved is a reflection
when two hearts become one
our lives intertwined like roses
blooming when the season comes.

-Jenni Bovetti

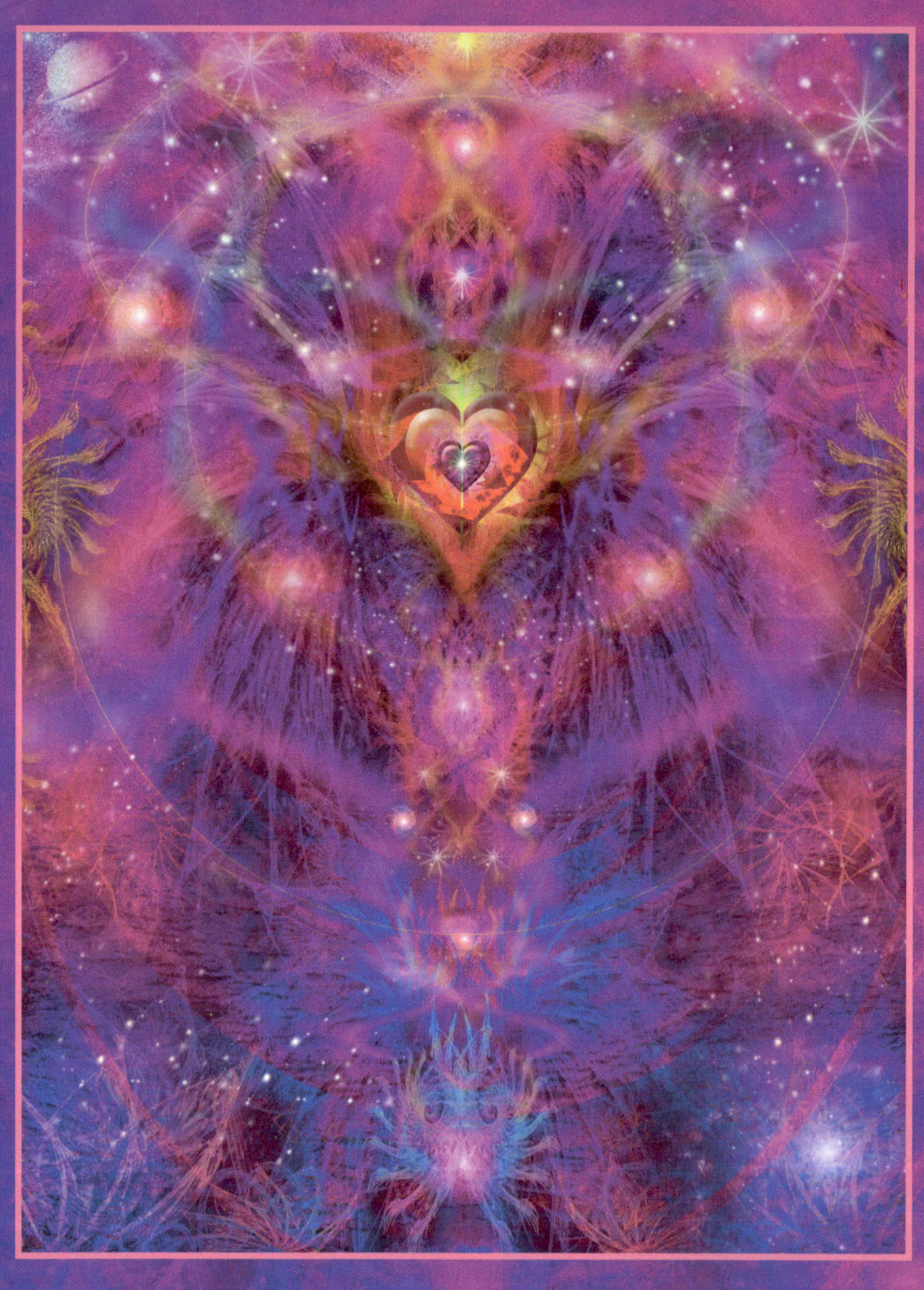

Create life

Rapture of Life
Caught in Love
Two Souls intertwined
Create Divine

D N A helix
conception of love
Tiny New Soul
cosmic of the above

-Alixandra Mullins

Fruits of Love

Two Souls unite
Love Divine
conception

Birth of Life
Fruit of Love
Joy Happiness
Complete

Miracle born
of love

-Alixandra Mullins

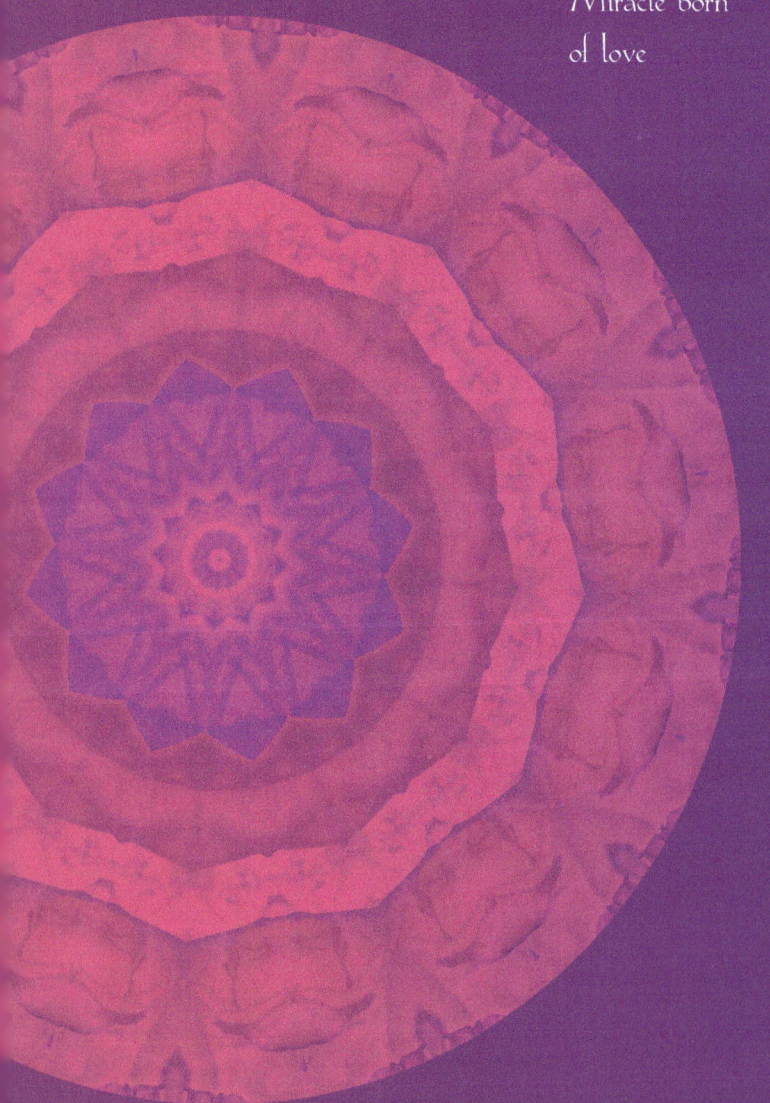

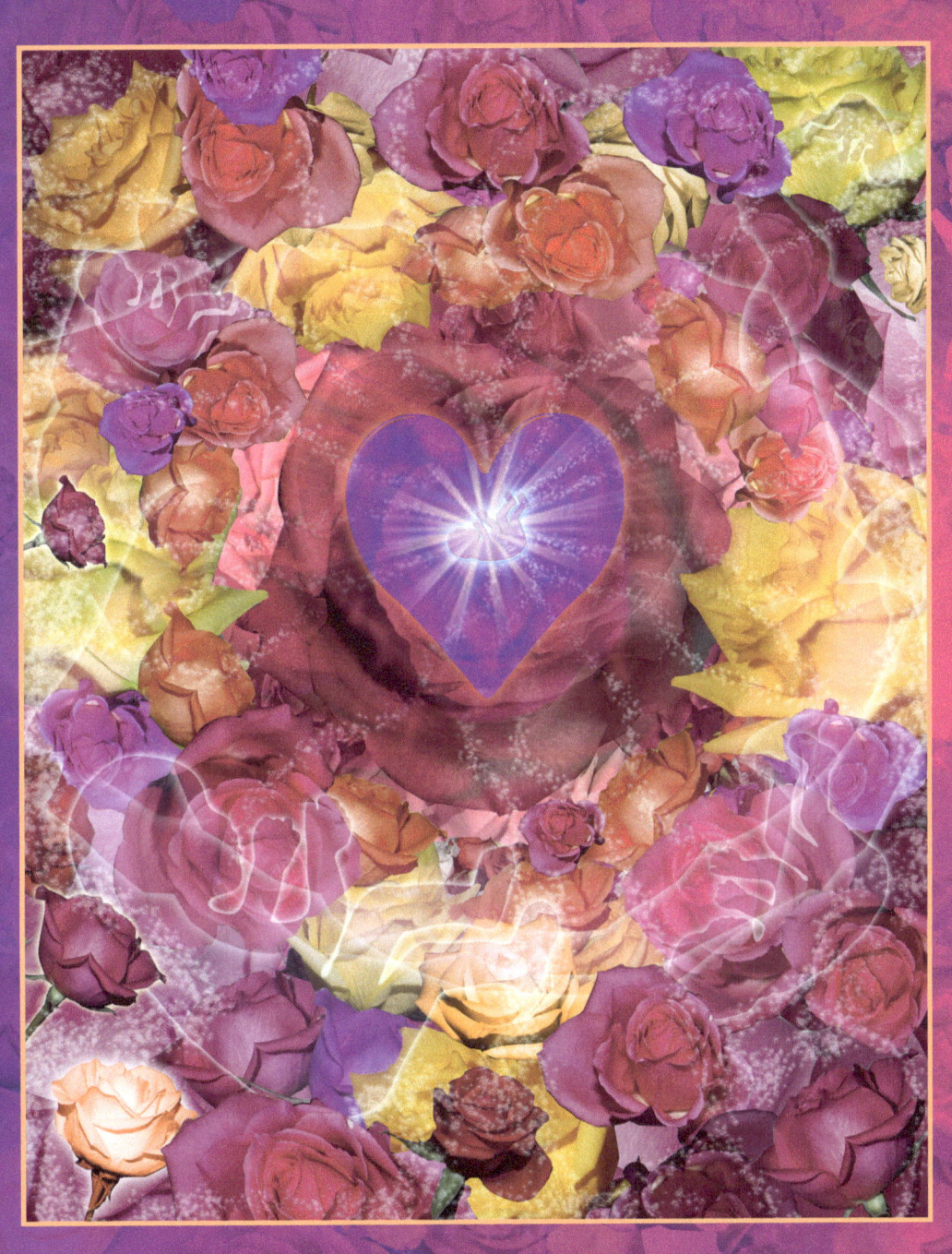

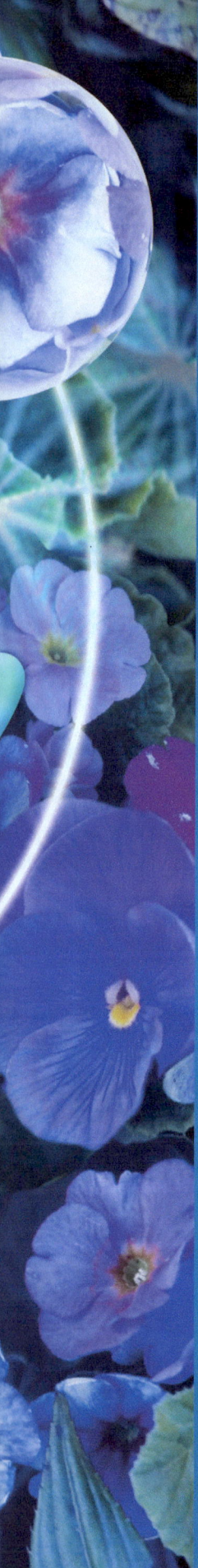

Paradise

Paradise exists
as Dusty Sand
a Full Moon high
Drumming Rhythms
And Fire Flies

Paradise exists
As Spinning over water
Reflecting high and low
Burning Water Nymphs
In the placid moon glow

Paradise exists
As a Dance of desire
to sweetly admire
holding intent
and subtly moving with fire

Paradise exists
Playful and innocent
a Jolt of perfection
With no descent

-Sequoia Ravenmoon

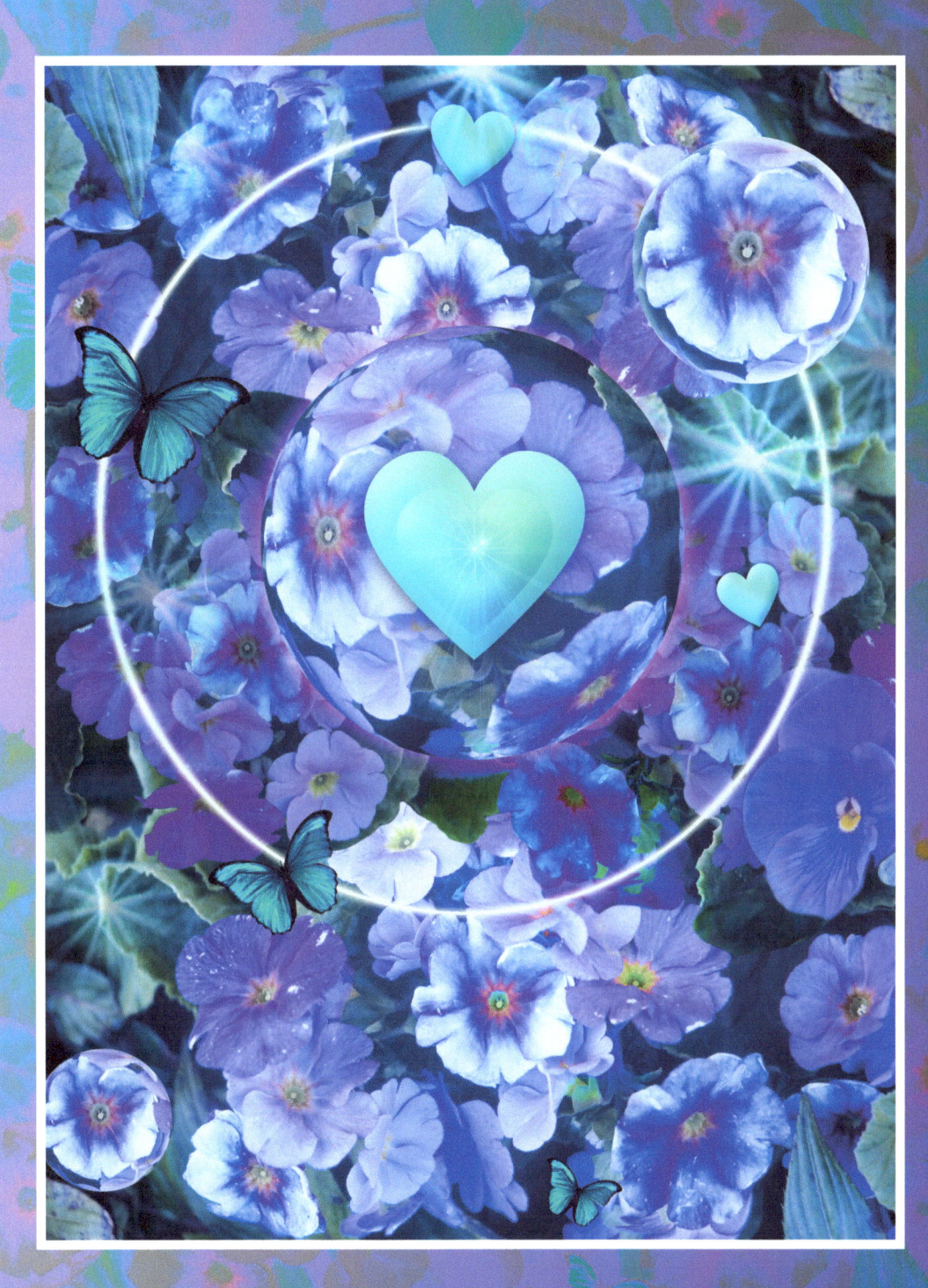

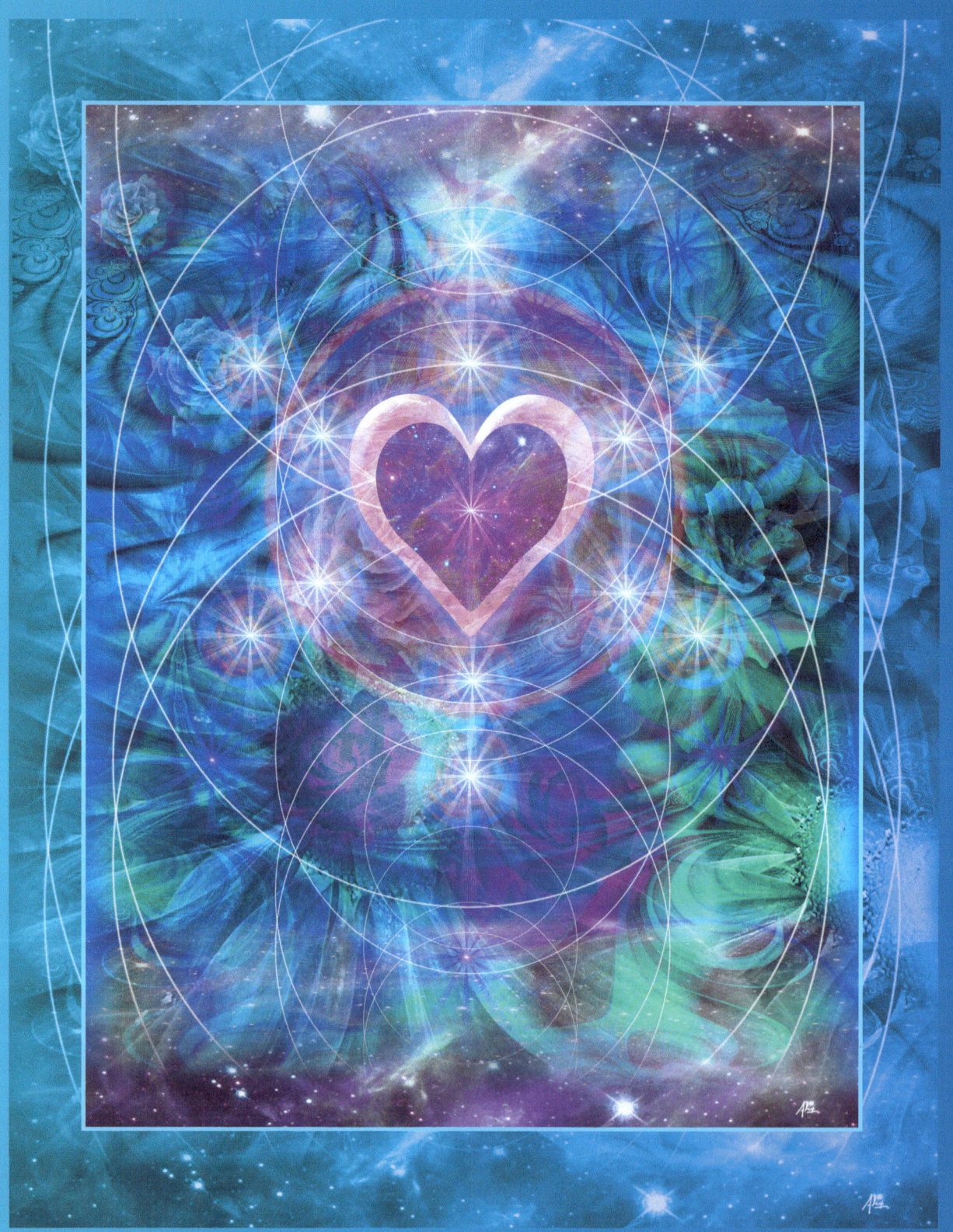

Beautiful Vision

A thousand petals of a luscious vision.

Caught deeply in the sensation of an instant connection.

Freely standing on a fast moving river.

Passionately screaming silent words of surrender.

Angel of bliss dances still in the night.

The wisdom of grace illuminates her sight.

In what direction the seer does go?

In what direction the knower does know?

Spiraling words two meanings could describe.

Too many questions to accurately decide.

There is No direction.

And there is NO return.

When your Eyes are open,

your vision discern.

Close your eyes and in darkness the truth you will perceive.

Dance freely, No worry, no retreat.

Faith in your destiny will keep you from sorrow.

As the angels delight in beauty you follow,

Dancing in divine thankfullness

For to them you are pure and eternal

Love

-Sequoia Ravenmoon

Dream

Oh Spectrum of Radiant Light

A Nightime beauty of incomprehensible sight

A Guardian of divinity to lead the way

The Rapture of beauty fading into yesterday

A Candlelit of faith in tomorrows unknown

The Edge of reality where wisdom has grown

Forever Alive in the abundant array

Forever united in the twilight of day

Caught In your reflection

Standing frozen in Time

Silent and still I breathe in your vision sublime.

- Sequoia Ravenmoon

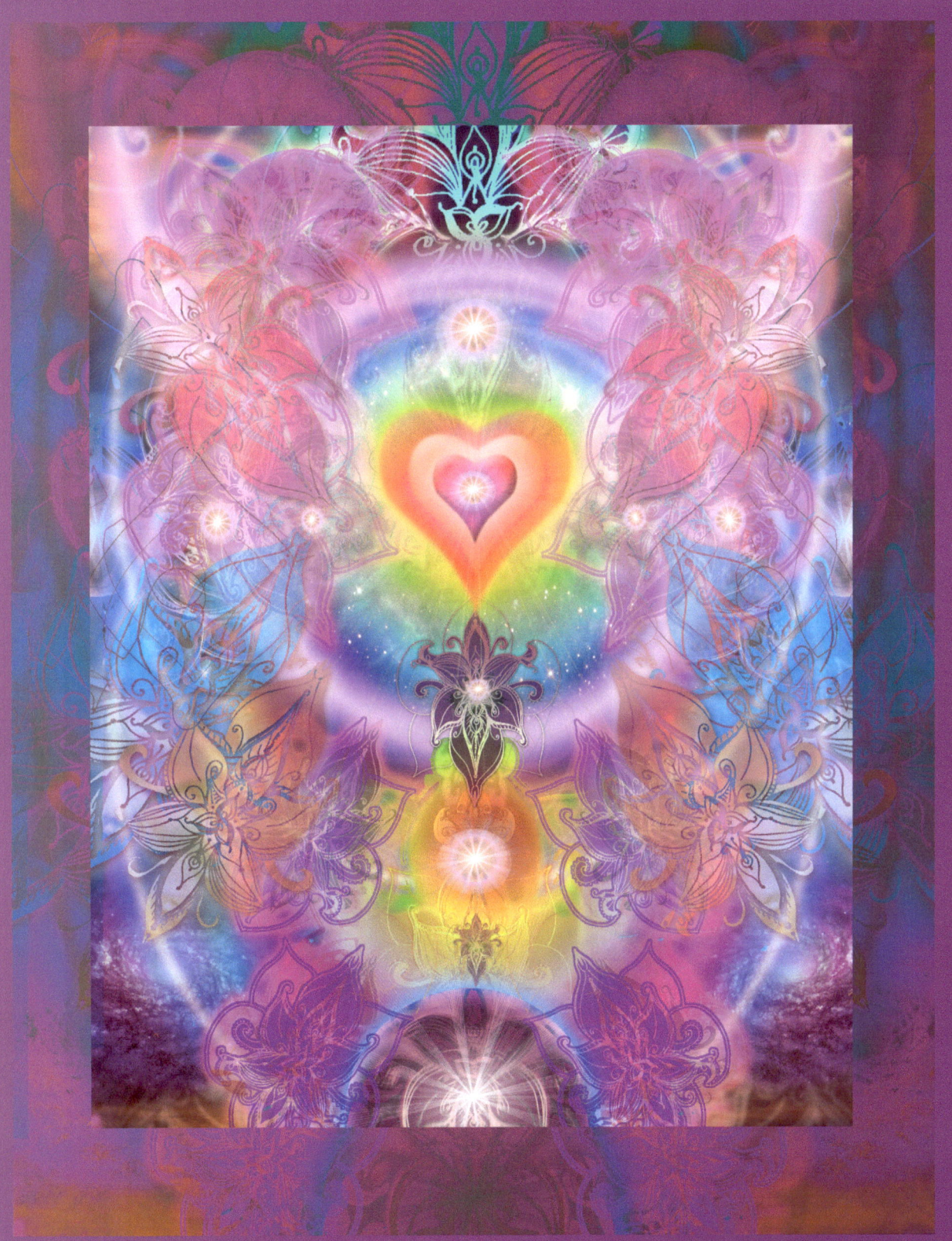

Garden of Love

Come my Love into the garden where I will be waiting

my Beloved is the fragrance of lavendar

breathing in my spirit becomes liquid,

soothing, calming, surrendering

receiving of my Lover's touch

flowing through my spine

intoxicating like the most expensive wine

heart opening radiating like the sun

love glowing from his eyes

reflecting like a mirror piercing my in most depths

seeing the Divine within as One

sweet are the kisses of his lips touching mine

leading down the sacred garden path

in the garden intertwining like the petals of the rose

fully opening with perfumed blossoms

I am his and he is mine in the garden of sacred love Divine

-Jenni Bovetti

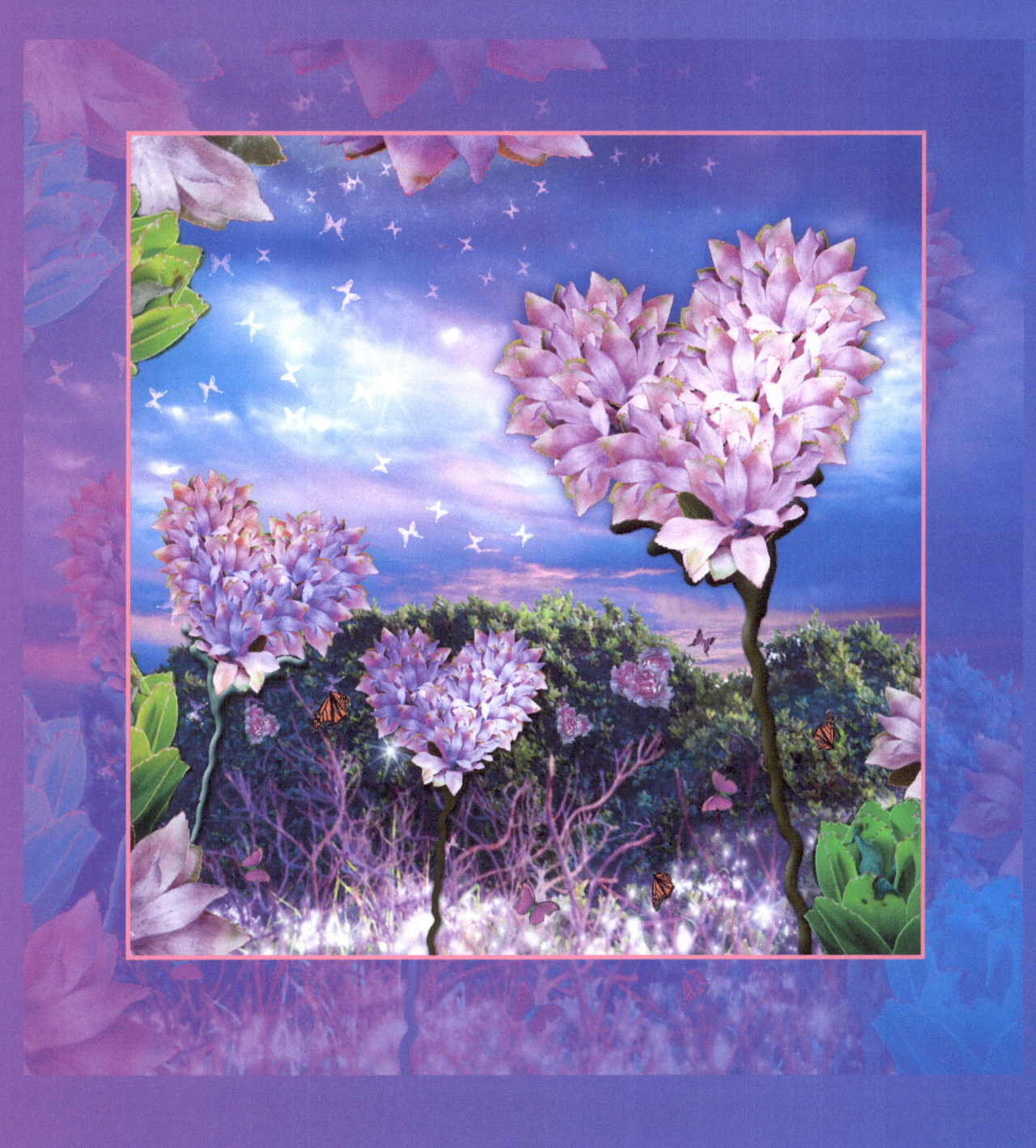

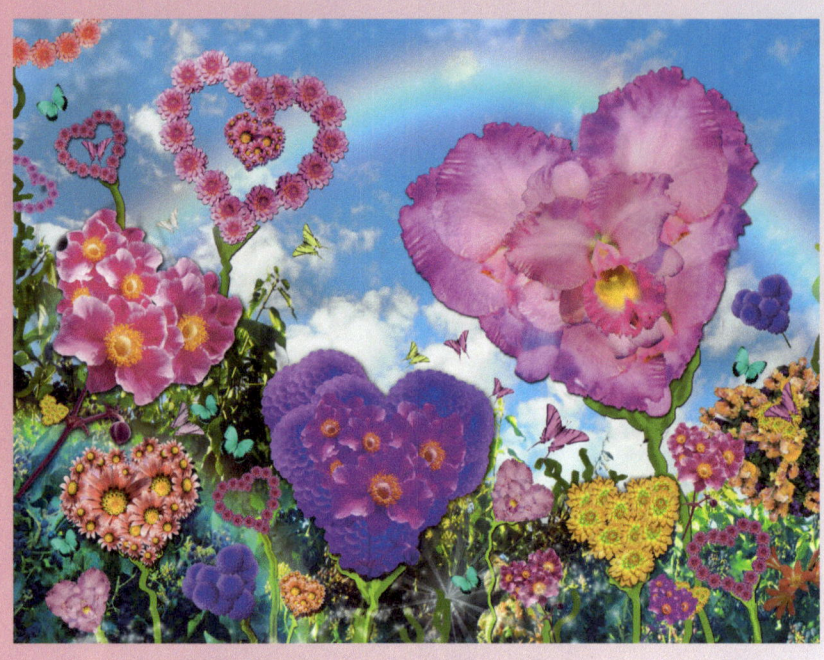

Garden of Love

She followed him
down a forgotten path
into the twilight evening
where they came upon a Garden

The LoveFlowers Bloom
as sparkling light
followed the lovers
into the morning sunlight

-Alixandra Mullins

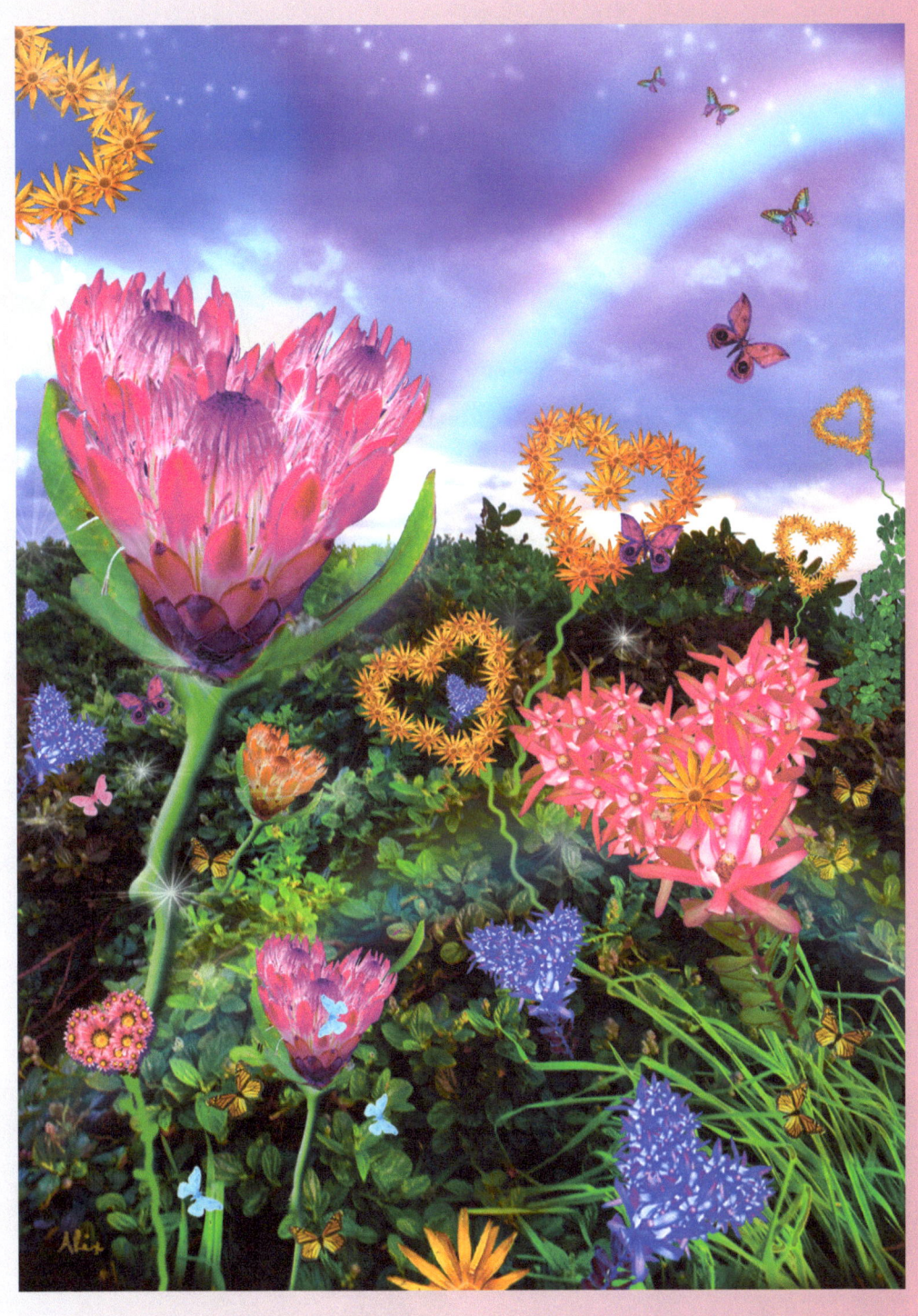

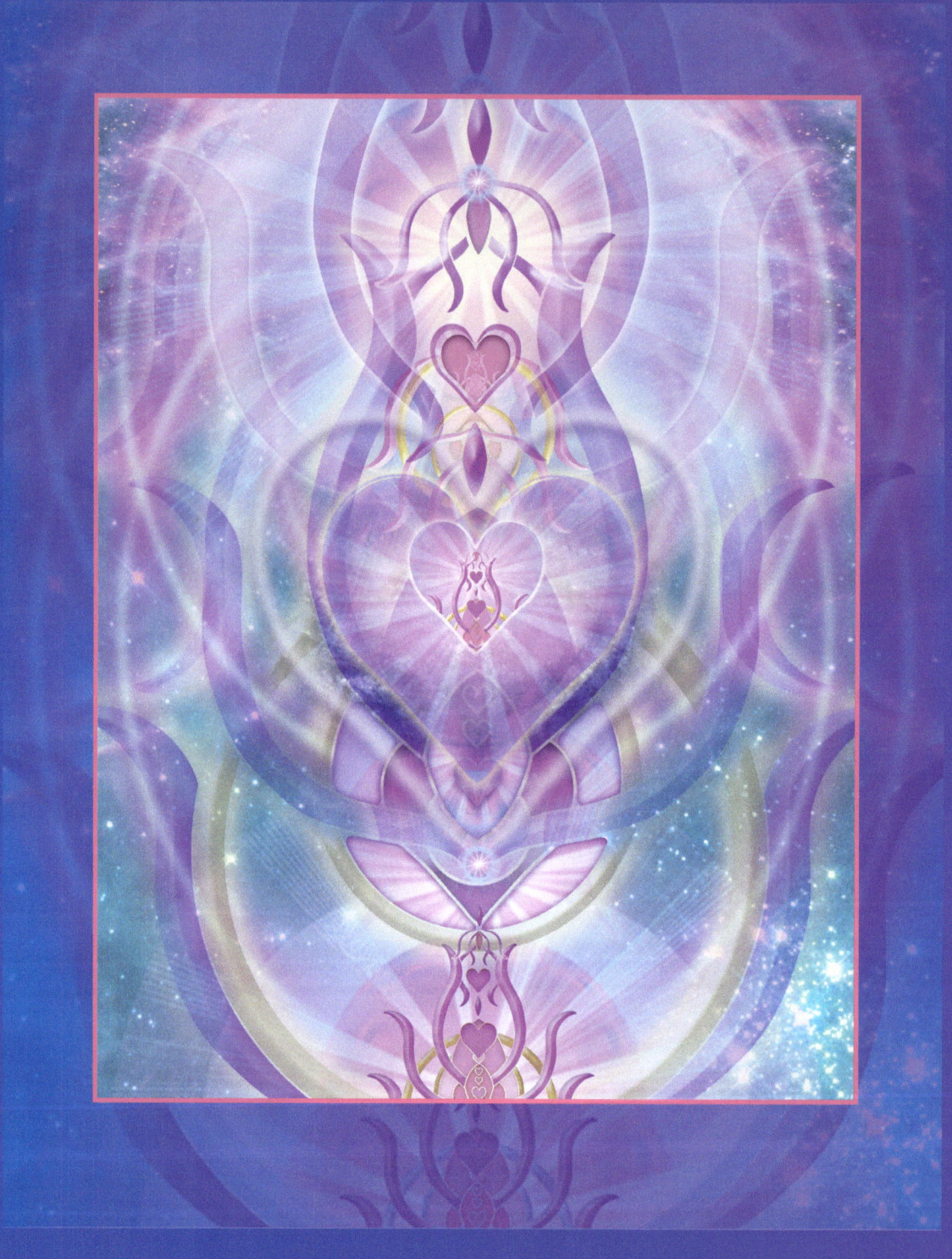

Love

the water which cleanses
the spirit
and brings peace
to the war-torn, the despaired
the broken-hearted
open the heart
to pour kindness
upon it
softening, tempering, rejuvenating
the soul
to meet
with
the one, the infinite
in healing
truth
balance
joy
tranquility
and love never ending

-Alixandra Mullins

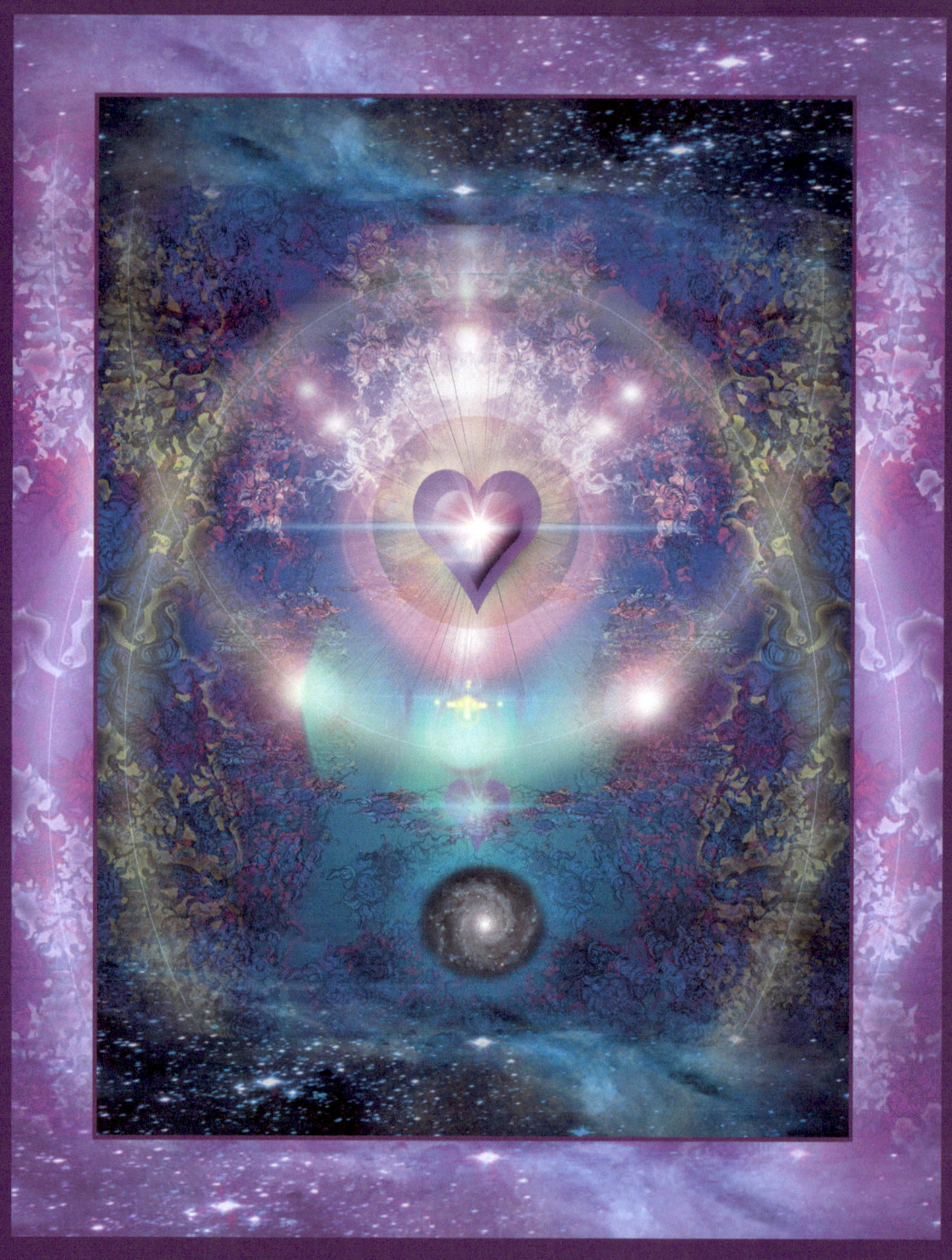

The Heart of the Universe

Infinite
Cosmos
links the soul
of humanity's echo
beyond the outer realmes
to divinity
where
calls to the angels
are listened
the entire
universe
of at one ness
still
as the web of life

love is connected

-Alixandra Mullins

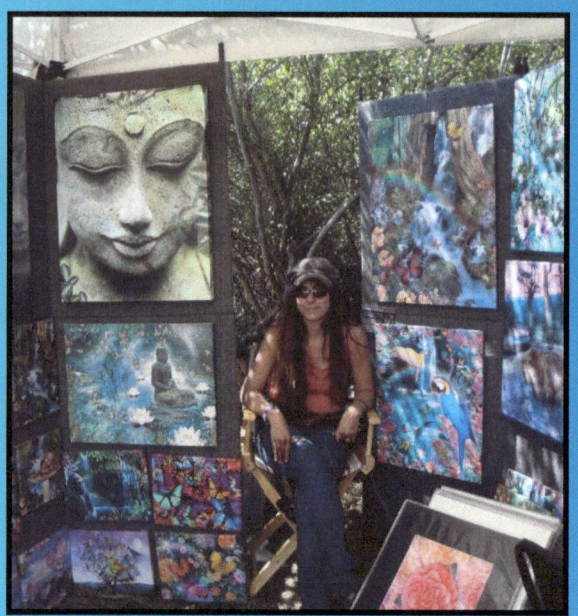

Artwork created by Alixandra Mullins

Alixandra Mullins has been drawing and creating various types of art since early childhood. She began with traditional painting and photography, then after discovering exciting new artist tools at the Digital Arts Center in Santa Barbara, California, she decided to explore the possibilities of art created with new technology. She earned a multimedia arts & technologies degree and another, more advanced degree in Digital Media from California State University Sacramento. She lives in Northern California, and wtih a deep love of nature, spend many hours photographing the outdoor world along the west coast and beyong. Inspired by the infinite potential of the digital darkroom and the artistic possibilities to combine various mediums such as photography, painting and graphic design into one image, alix continues to create work in this collage style. She synergistically creates a new composition through the use of digital collage. Creating art bordering on surreal, magical and sometimes mythical realm between dreams, spirit and the raw natural world. Alix is also a dancer, piano player,and a writer of stories and poetry. *http://alixandramullins.com*

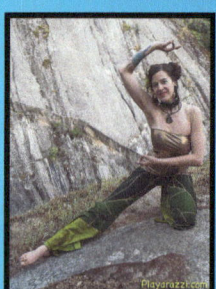

Poetry contributed by: Sequoia Raven Moon

Sequoia Raven Moon is a self taught artist whose roots grow deep in the elements of the natural world. Her main creative influences come through her connections with music, dance, nature, and travelling. Through her ART, Sequoia, expresses the colorful and abstract realities of life. Weaving together many facets of her creative explorations, she shares a poetic texture rich with melodic vibrations. Her creations are an alchemical process that pulsate through all aspects of life and are represented as a collection of the pieces of her HART. Sequoia's Art works are made using creative re-use whenever possible. Her mediums include: Poetry, Painting, Drawing, Photo/Videography, and Dance. *http://sacredfiredance.com*

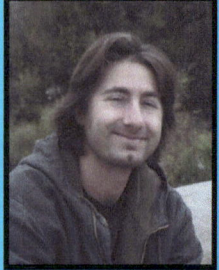

Poetry contributed by: Gregory Mullins

Greg Mullins has been writing poetry and stories for most of his life. He draws inspiration from the natural world and meditation. He teaches Yoga and Tai Chi and finds the essence of all arts in everyday activities.

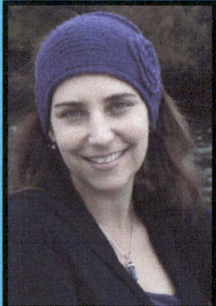

Poetry contributed by: Jenni Bovetti

Jenni Bovetti is a teacher and mother. She writes out of joy and wonder at the beauty of the divine, and its reflection in loving human relationships. She is a Yoga teacher who encourages others to breathe deeply and experience life to the fullest.

All artwork featured in this book is available as a canvas print, which is handstretched by the artist,and hand embellished glazed acrylic paint Artwork can be purchased online at *www.alixandramullins.com*

www.ingramcontent.com/pod-product-compliance
Lightning Source LLC
Chambersburg PA
CBHW040753200526
45159CB00025B/2086